Treat Him Like a Dog

(And Other Tips for Marital Bliss)

Treat Him Like a Dog

(And Other Tips for Marital Bliss)

MARK GUNGOR | JENNA MC CARTHY

TREAT HIM LIKE A DOG
(And Other Tips for Marital Bliss)
BY MARK GUNGOR AND JENNA MC CARTHY

Illustrations by Daria Tarawneh
Book design by Debbie Bishop

Special thanks to Diane Brierley, Larry Patterson and Mary Seipel for contributing their time and effort in the writing of this book.

©Copyright 2019 Mark Gungor.
All rights reserved worldwide under the Pan-American and International Copyright Conventions.

For information address inquiries to: info@laughyourway.com

www.markgungor.com

Scripture quotations taken from The Holy Bible, New International Version [R] NIV [R] Copyright [C] 1973, 1978, 1984, 2011 by Biblica, Inc. [TM] Used by permission. All rights reserved worldwide.

Printed in Poland

Wydawnictwo ARKA
Blogocka 28
43-400 Cieszyn, Polska
www.arkadruk.pl

To all the women who desire to improve
their relationships and have been convinced it is
much more complicated than it actually is.

Treat Him Like a Dog
(And Other Tips for Marital Bliss)

Contents

Introduction	v
Treat Him Like a Dog	11
Treat Him Like a Boss	19
Treat Him Like an Employee	27
Treat Him Like a Gynecologist	35
Treat Him Like a Cab Driver	45
Treat Him Like a Child	57
Treat Him Like a Personal Trainer	65
Treat Him Like Your Phone	75
Treat Him Like a Stranger	81
BONUS CHAPTER! Do NOT Treat Him Like Your Girlfriend	91

Treat Him Like a Dog

MARK GUNGOR | JENNA MC CARTHY

Introduction

MARK GUNGOR | JENNA MC CARTHY

Introduction

Congratulations! You're now the proud owner of another book on relationships. We keep buying them because we want to succeed with the people closest to us. I should say, "Women keep buying them…" The truth is, most men would rather have root canal surgery or a rectal exam than read a book on relationships. Not that they don't need the help, and not that they wouldn't benefit from the wisdom and insight this book is teeming with. Oh, they neeeeeeed the help all right. But since it's the women who typically purchase and read relationship books, this work will be addressed to the fairer sex.

When you stood before that altar (the first draft

Treat Him Like a Dog

of this work had a typo and the word was spelled 'alter'. I laughed and thought, "Oh, they're about to be altered alright...") or beside those gently lapping waves on that blinding white beach of your wedding-destination dreams, you said some version of the following:

"I promise to love,
honor and cherish
you in sickness
and in health,
for richer or for poorer,
for better or for worse,
till death do us part."

You did! You said that!

As it turns out, *till death do us part* is a really looooong time—and being a loving, honoring, cherishing spouse all day every day is no easy feat. In fact, by most accounts it borders on the impossible. Not to mention that living with another person (which typically means sharing the same bed, the same bathroom and the same thermostat) has been known to try even the most temperate of tempers.

If you're among the very blessed, you're not bickering about the Big Things (namely money, sex and kids) on a daily basis. Most married couples admit that more often than not they find themselves arguing about tiny, trivial matters. Solomon once wrote:

> *A quarrelsome wife is like the dripping*
> *of a leaky roof in a rainstorm.*
> Proverbs 27:15 NIV

Granted, that was written from a man's perspective and there is conveniently no mention of the major pain in the rear that a husband can be, but the image of a *dripping, leaky roof* pretty much summarizes what life can be like after the "I Dos" have echoed off into the distant horizon.

He left crumbs in the sink *again!* He forgot to pick up the dry cleaning like you asked him to! And who puts the empty milk carton back in the refrigerator, anyway? These are just a few from the long list of transgressions he commits on a continual basis as he demonstrates his skillful ability to descend into pig-like behavior. *Drip, drip, drip.*

Treat Him Like a Dog

The truth is, many of us –men included—willingly (sometimes even eagerly) pick a fight with our spouses over some petty thing that if it were committed by almost *anyone else in the world*, we'd graciously let it slide. That's what *dripping* will do to you.

Part of the problem is that pesky living-together-business. When you're confined to a small space (relative to the rest of the planet, let's say), the people who share that space with you get front row seats to your every emotional extreme: They are there to witness your rapturous highs (You got the promotion! Your hair looks amazing today!) and your heartbreaking lows (Your beloved dog has to be put down! You gained four pounds on your diet!). The highs often go by without a lot of fanfare, but those lows? They kick you in the butt every time.

Here's why: Just for fun, let's look at the dying-dog scenario. (After all, nothing lifts the spirits like a lively discussion about the death of the family pet.)

Seriously, tragic things happen in our lives on a discouragingly regular basis. But you still have to show up at work, and maybe attend a PTA meeting, and possibly meet with the accountant or play another rousing game of Candy Land, and essentially do all manner of challenging, grown-up things that require you to keep it together when inside you're a miserable mess.

So you do—you keep it together brilliantly, in fact. At least until you get home. And then you fall apart, because you're not a machine and sometimes you have to let it out. (After all, you miss that stupid dog - that dog that regularly added to your already heavy work load each and every day.) And who's left staring at the broken pieces of you and scratching his head as to how to begin to put you back together again? No, it's not all the king's horses and all the king's men; it's that person you promised to love, honor and cherish every single day for the rest of ever. (Honestly! What were you thinking?)

Here's the thing: We're not bad people; far from it. We're human. We have value. God loves us all. (How and why, I'll never understand. I mean, let's face it, this would be a great planet if it weren't for people.) And it's human nature to take things for granted. There's actually a scientific name for it—hedonic adaptation—but I'll spare you the psychology lecture. The bottom

Treat Him Like a Dog

line is that we don't appreciate the things that become commonplace in our lives.

For instance, being able to sit painlessly at a desk until you throw out your back and get laid up for a week. Or when was the last time you gave your thumb a second thought? Slice that thing open with your sharpest butcher knife and have it bandaged up for a month and I guarantee, you'll be grateful to have it back. How about breathing? Inhale, exhale, inhale, exhale; you do it all day long, never considering the fact that your hardworking respiratory system is very busy keeping you alive while you're off playing tennis and surfing the Internet or steaming broccoli.

So it goes with your husband. Sure you love him, in the vague and all-encompassing sense of the word. You honor him, especially when he takes out the trash without being asked. You try your best to cherish him, even when his snoring wakes you up for the third time in a single night. But you don't always *appreciate* him—and he certainly doesn't always get the best version of you.

How can he, when there's a big, demanding world out there that wants—often *needs*—more than you've got to give in the first place? Think of your time, attention and affection as a glorious holiday meal to which you've invited pretty much *everyone in your entire contact list.* You get dressed to the nines, polish a truckload of silver and then heap their plates high, because you're a gracious hostess and it's what you've been taught to do. You smile and you make polite chitchat as you serve your parade of hungry guests. Hours pass. Your lipstick is long gone and your feet are beginning to throb and all you want is for this party to end and these people to go home. At the very end of the line is your husband. He's starving; he's lonely; he's missed you all day. But you're exhausted, out of food, and your face hurts from smiling. If he's lucky, you might toss him the nearly naked turkey carcass to pick over before you hobble into bed.

If it were but one giant holiday meal a year where your husband got the sad leftovers, it would be one thing. But many wives are living that scenario day in and day out. If you are like most women, you smile at strangers on the street all day long, praise your kids for every scribbled stick person they draw and fawn

Treat Him Like a Dog

over your dog for lifting a lousy paw. (Of course I just had to remind you of the stupid dead dog.) Think your husband wouldn't like a piece of that action? Think again. I know, you're already *giving till it hurts*. But sometimes it's good to step back and take a look at some of the people and things in your life that get the sort of time and attention from you that your husband would give his eyeteeth to enjoy.

It's also crucial to understand that what is the most *important* doesn't always get the most *time*. For example, we've all heard the standard priority list: God first, then spouse, children and work. Sounds about right. But think about it – you actually spend the most time working, family gets your next biggest allotment, your spouse gets crumbs (until the kids grow up and finally leave) and God? Well, who prays eight hours a day? Still, the priority list is right. But you see, it's not about the amount of time – it's about quality and devotion. Since what is most important actually ends up with the least amount of our time, it is up to us to make sure that time matters.

So, since this book is dedicated to sharing simple bits of advice about how you can continue to care for and cherish that man you pledged your heart to and because I don't want you to be traumatized for life, I'll start with your healthy, happy dog. (The dead dog analogy was getting old anyway...)

MARK GUNGOR | JENNA MC CARTHY

Treat Him Like a Dog

Treat Him Like a Dog

People joke about it all the time: "If there's such a thing as reincarnation, I hope I come back as a dog." (Personally, I think the concept of reincarnation is a major bummer. I mean, who wants to do this again??!! Learning not to poop in your pants. English class with Mrs. Northrup! And puberty? Again with all the zits?? I don't think so...) But seriously, dogs get treated better than most people I know.

When you come home from work at the end of a long day, you probably wouldn't dream of brushing past little Fido with a curt 'hey,' or immediately launching into a detailed account of your terrible, horrible, no good, very bad day. Not in a million years! You'll drop

Treat Him Like a Dog

your keys, your bags, your worries, your children if you're not thinking clearly, and pull that lovable little ball of fur straight into your arms and lavish love on him until you're breathless. You let him lick your face and you don't even tell him his breath stinks! When he's fast asleep, you marvel at how gosh-darned-adorable he is as you tiptoe ever so quietly around his bed, desperate not to disturb his precious slumber.

And think about how you talk to Fido: Come, sit, stay, fetch, drop. You don't give this simple creature endless, complicated commands or confuse him with long-winded explanations of *why* you want him to fetch the ball or *how much it hurts your feelings* when you ask him to sit and he doesn't. You talk to him the way *he* needs to be talked to; not the way *you* prefer to converse. Why? Because you're wise enough to realize that doing anything else would be the ultimate exercise in futility. And you realize that the poor creature will just never think like you! *Think about that for a minute.* Women often get frustrated because their guys don't act, think, respond and feel the way they do. Just ask most women to describe their ideal man and listen to the response: They invariably describe another woman! "I want a man who will share his feelings." "I want a man who loves to go shopping." "I want a man who cleans up after himself without having to be asked." "I want a man who is sensitive to the needs around him and doesn't have to be prodded." Seriously?? Sounds like they are more interested in finding a new girlfriend. But I digress.

Take a minute to consider the reward system you've set up for your pooch. When he does what you ask him to do, you rub him and pet him and tell him he's *such a good boy.* When he doesn't get it the first time? You patiently (that part is really key) go through the motions again, dozens of times if necessary, offering up treats and encouragement for even a whisper of compliance, a *hint* that he might be on the path to success. (By the way ladies, you actually *can* train a man. All studies have shown that women improve men. According to the data, married men are happier, healthier, make more money and actually live longer than single men. Women do improve men, but you have to think of him as a long-term project. The good news: You can eventually get a man to where you want him. The bad news: Then he dies.)

Treat Him Like a Dog

But back to Fido: Every once in a while, your precious pup messes up. Big time. He poops on the living room rug, wakes the baby with his barking, gets your brand new shoe confused with a T-bone. Are you mad? Sure! Do you let him know? Absolutely. Do you simmer and stew and give him the death-stare-silent-treatment for days on end waiting for him to drop to your feet with an overwrought apology and a promise that it will never, ever happen again? Of course not. You explain what he did, you forgive him and you move on.

Simple as that.

And don't forget all of the tiny little things you do for Fido—Fido who asks for nothing and expects even less. You buy him fluffy toys and cuddly blankets and outrageously cute collars for the simple reason that doing so brings you joy. You walk him in the rain, sacrificing your hairdo if you have to, because Fido needs his exercise, and that is far more important than your vanity. You save him a few bites of your steak because you know it will make him giddy, and sometimes you toss him a bone just because he's so stinking cute. Imagine what would happen if every once in a while you rubbed and petted your husband, told him he was *such a good boy* and you know... tossed him an unexpected bone (if you know what I mean).

"*But dogs are easy to love,*" I can hear you crying. I agree, they are. They really are. But men are pretty easy to love, too – if you're willing to take the time to understand them – just like you do with your dog. And dogs and people have a remarkable thing in common: With both species, you get back what you give.

MARK GUNGOR | JENNA MC CARTHY

Treat Him Like a Boss

Treat Him Like a Dog

Treat Him Like a Boss

Few things can get a woman more fired up today than the notion that she should "obey" her husband. I know, I know... the wedding vows of old used that word and it's even found in the Bible.

Consider what that phrase really means for a moment... Because let's face it: Word meanings change over time. I remember when bad was bad, but now if you're really bad you're cool - which used to mean you were cold - which now means you are hip. Uuuugh...

One would be hard-pressed to find a more offensive word today than the word "obey." It has connotations more in line with slavery than marriages of equals or even normal human interactions.

Treat Him Like a Dog

I would argue that a better word today would be the word "listen." If a child is being problematic, he or she is told by the mother that they need to "listen." If a teenager is driving the mom nuts, the father is most likely to jump in with, "Listen to your mother."

A boss or supervisor would never walk into an office and demand "You have to obey me!" (That would, most likely, lead to a law suit.) No, a boss or supervisor would simply encourage the employees to be careful to "listen to and follow the instructions."

I think the new translations of the Bible would better serve the language of today if they used the word "listen" rather than "obey." Most contemporary translations no longer use words that are now considered offensive - words like ass, bastard or piss (just check out the old King James Version). Today's translators are careful to avoid using those words since the meanings have shifted to be pretty offensive. Well, I would argue the same should be done with the word "obey."

When I say *treat your husband like a boss*, I do not mean to imply in any way, shape or form that he is the Southern slave master and you are Kunta Kinte. I am merely suggesting that you give your husband the same basic respect and consideration you give to your boss. (Let me interject here that each and every time I refer to your boss or higher-up, I'm going to go out on a limb and assume this is a person whom you hold in only the highest regard. Certainly, no one wants you to start treating your husband the way you treat the kind of superior you'd push down the escalator if you thought you could get away with it.)

No matter what job you have—whether it's heart surgeon or homemaker—there's undoubtedly a hierarchy in place. Even if you're at the tippy-top of that chain of command, you're expected to be accountable to somebody. I remember when I became the owner of my own company. I thought, "Finally, I don't have to listen to any idiot telling me what to do!" Well, it didn't take long to realize I was answering to all kinds of idiots: my customers. No one escapes having to listen to someone else.

If you're the hospital chief of staff, you're answering to the chairman or dean. If you're the CEO of a Fortune 500 company, you're answering to the shareholders. If you're the President, you answer to the people. Why do you stay accountable? For one thing,

Treat Him Like a Dog

you don't want to lose your job. For another, it's a sign of respect.

I'm certainly not proposing that we revert to the patriarchal fetch-me-my-slippers-and-pipe days. But think about how you act toward your boss, that person to whom you're expected to be accountable. I'm going to guess that you listen to this person and try your best for that person... even if you wholeheartedly believe that at times what he or she is asking of you is a pointless waste of time and six or seven miles beneath you. You probably do these menial, meaningless tasks with a smile. Perhaps a painful smile, but smiling nonetheless. The boss asks you to drop her shirts off at the dry cleaner on your way home? Can do! Stay an hour late to edit the report she promised to get to you three days ago? No problem! Drive his mother-in-law to the airport? He may be pushing it here—but he'll never know it. Why? Because it's your *job* to listen to him.

If you're getting all prickly at the notion of it being *your job to listen to your husband*, let me point out that this is the act of a heart of faith. Again, I'm not talking about the bossing-around sort of obedience; I'm simply asking you to believe in, respect and, yes, listen to your husband! Afford him the same kind of energy and respect you show to your stupid boss – even when you know your boss is stupid. Now, I am not implying you must do everything like some kind of non-thinking robot. Even with your boss, you don't have to do *everything*. If he or she is abusive or asks you to break the law or puts you in a very uncomfortable position, you just say no. Respectfully, but you still say no.

Let me ask you this: Has your boss ever, even one time, witnessed you in a hormonal rage or heard you slam a door, mutter insults under your breath or tick off a list of how much more you do around the office than she does? I'm betting that she hasn't. Do you criticize the way she does *her* job, and accuse her—angrily, with your head spinning Linda Blair-style—of not appreciating you often or enthusiastically enough? I'm going to guess that the answer is: No.

Aretha definitely knew what she was talking about; it really does come down to R-E-S-P-E-C-T. I get it: Respect is a two-way street. But at the end of the day you can only control what you do (and hope he follows suit).

Give respect and listen just like you have always

Treat Him Like a Dog

done to the bosses you've answered to all your life. "But what if I don't agree with him?!" Oh, I don't have a problem with the normal disagreements of life and, despite this analogy, I get that your husband is not actually your boss. I also get that you can always just quit your job and tell your boss to stick it and get another job. (A bit more complicated in marriage - to say the least.) I'm just suggesting that if you treat your man with the same kind of intentional respect you give your boss, you would find yourself having much greater success with him.

To obey implies you have no option but to do what you are told. Listening, on the other hand, shows respect even if there is disagreement. You can always "listen" even when you don't always agree - even if you won't always go along. If a man feels he is being treated with the courtesy and respect of being heard, he can usually handle an opposing view—without even having to involve Human Resources.

MARK GUNGOR | JENNA MC CARTHY

Treat Him Like an Employee

Treat Him Like a Dog

Treat Him Like an Employee

Imagine this: You've just been elected President of the United States. Yes, you; the POTUS! (Quit mentally redecorating the White House and picturing your trendsetting new hairdo; there'll be time for that later.) After the champagne is popped and the confetti settles, your brand new Vice President turns to you eagerly.

Veep: What do you want to do first?

You [bursting into tears]: Really? After all the time campaigning together, you don't *know* what I want? What was I thinking, doing this with you? [Runs dramatically from Oval Office.]

Okay, I exaggerate. A *little*. But we—and by "we"

Treat Him Like a Dog

I mean all of us, men included—often expect our spouses to be mind-readers. Which would rank up there with winning the lottery or waking up with six-pack abs. Unfortunately, having a mind-reading spouse is probably less likely to happen than either of those things.

As the boss—whether your position is the newly crowned leader of the free world, the CFO of a telecommunications conglomerate or the manager of a donut shop—your job is to guide your team; to instruct them; to give them clear, detailed instructions and lay out your very specific expectations of them. Sounds pretty obvious, right?

Let's imagine you just hired a talented new team member named Jane. You searched high and low before finally settling on Jane, and you're pretty proud of your choice. After all, there was no shortage of qualified candidates. But ultimately you chose Jane above all of the others because she was both skilled and eager to please. Now that Jane is on the job, how do you manage her?

Well, for one thing, if there's a task you want done, (and this is revolutionary stuff here) *you tell her precisely what it is*. You don't lurk in her shadow hoping she'll see the papers that need to be filed or remember the calls that need to be made. "I'd like you to be here by nine," you tell Jane, and you rarely pout or cross your arms when you say it. When Jane tells you she's all caught up with her work and asks for her next assignment, you probably don't groan, "You know what? Never mind. I'll just do it *myself.*"

Consider this: Even though you have very specific expectations for Jane, when she does what you feel is required of her, you praise her. When she lands a new account for the company or discovers a way to cut back on your overhead, you might even give her a bonus. (Everyone loves an unexpected bonus!) What you don't do is withhold any recognition whatsoever because, frankly, you know you're doing so much more than she is—and it's not like anybody is giving *you* any trophies.

Now let's suppose—purely for argument's sake—that Jane is late for work one day. Do you fly off the handle, berate her in front of her co-workers or give her the cold shoulder for four days? Of course you don't! "I'm going to need you to arrive on time," you'll tell her simply, your words forceful but kind. Why? Because you are wise enough to know that when you treat your employees with respect, they are far more motivated to

Treat Him Like a Dog

want to please you.

Here's the thing about us guys: When you say "I really want you to do more around here" or "I could use more help" we have absolutely no idea what this means. We're simple creatures; we need you to be s-p-e-c-i-f-i-c.

"But why can't he see what needs to be done?!?" you moan. Let's face it girls: What *you* think needs to be done and what *he* thinks needs to be done can be two very different worlds. "But why is he such a slob?!?" I don't know – maybe it's his mother's fault. Maybe he's clueless. Or maybe he is just an actual slob and it's hardwired in his DNA. Let's face it, a lot of guys could live like hamsters – wad up some paper – sleep there, poop there, he's done.

And what difference does it make what you think he *should* or *should not* intuitively be aware of anyway? Just like you don't sit around and wait for your employees to have an epiphany of what needs to be done, more often than not, he's going to need to be told.

But let's be honest here – a lot of women don't just want their guys to do something; they want them to *want* to do it. Well, here's a revelation for you girls: *We don't want to do it!* If we wanted to do it, we would have done it already!! (And don't forget that most guys are working their tails off already, just like you, often for very little praise or acknowledgement, I'll add.)

Besides, why do you care what he wants or doesn't want? You wouldn't care what your employees' heart motives were, would you? You'd just clearly point out what needs to be done – period. Now, if you say, "I'd like you to take out the trash," it is highly likely he will take out the trash. (Although I won't lie, a couple of reminders will most likely be needed. Let's face it, ladies: Asking a man to do something once is like never having asked him to do it at all! And don't forget, despite this analogy, he really *isn't* your employee.) Sure, you could waste lots of emotional energy being frustrated that he doesn't notice that the trash needs to be taken out... or you could cut to the chase and let him know what you'd like him to do. Help *him* help you... you know what I'm saying?

If you consistently treat your husband the way you'd treat your devoted, hardworking office assistant, I can almost promise you that you'll get those jobs done with a smile.

MARK GUNGOR | JENNA MC CARTHY

Treat Him Like a Gynecologist

Treat Him Like a Dog

MARK GUNGOR | JENNA MC CARTHY

Treat Him Like a Gynecologist

If there's a topic that makes both genders squirm uncomfortably, it would have to be S-E-X. And the truth is, it shouldn't! Sex is a lovely, beautiful thing—as long as you're getting it, that is. When you're *not* getting it (or giving it), it becomes a source of tension, resentment and frustration in your marriage.

As a pastor, I've never understood the Christian reluctance to discuss the issue of sex. I was doing a radio interview once on a Christian station and just before we went live with the broadcast, the lady conducting the interview looked straight at me in all seriousness and warned, "You're not going to use the 'S' word, are you?" I was a bit shocked as I thought to myself, "Now, why

Treat Him Like a Dog

in the world would I say sh*t on the air?" Suddenly it dawned on me: She meant the word sex! As if the word itself was filthy and dirty.

If there is one thing God is comfortable discussing, it is the subject of sex. When speaking of Israel's unfaithfulness to God, look at what God says to the Prophet Ezekiel:

There she lusted after her lovers, whose genitals were like those of donkeys and whose emission was like that of horses. So you longed for the lewdness of your youth, when in Egypt your bosom was caressed and your young breasts fondled. - Ezekiel 23:20 & 21 NIV

Whoa! Apparently God is not bashful talking about sex! So since we've all agreed that we're going to be comfortable talking about sex, here's a little newsflash for you: Men and women are wired completely differently in just about every way. And in no way is this dissimilarity more pronounced than when it comes to loving each other in the biblical sense.

Women typically take the following stance:

"Well, if he'd be *nicer* to me, and pick up his stinky gym clothes, and maybe plan a date night every once in a while, I'd be much more interested in being intimate with him."

To which the men reply: "If she'd just give it up without making me beg for it like a dog, I'd be so nice to her, her head would spin!"

(They say that, I promise.)

Remember those vows you took? For better or for worse, in sickness and in health, for richer or for poorer, *forsaking all others*? Well, he remembers them, too. And when he gave up the chance of getting naked with any other woman on the planet ever again, he was sort of hoping he'd be getting the frequent opportunity to be naked with you.

This isn't just me saying so. In survey after survey, when men are asked what makes them happiest in their marriages, "knowing my wife finds me attractive" ranks at the top. And how do we know you find us attractive? By wanting to get naked with us, of course!

(Again, simple creatures we are.)

In the tongue-in-cheek vein of "Treat Him Like a Dog," you know who most men would swap places with in a New York minute if given the chance? Your gynecologist. It's true! You schedule time with her and

Treat Him Like a Dog

you show up ready to do what needs to be done. She asks you to take your pants off and you do it with a smile. You don't pretend to be asleep or whine about your head hurting or launch into an hour-long account of the lousy day you had or tell her maybe you'll come back tomorrow because you ate too much at breakfast and you're a little bloated. Never once have you pretended to enjoy your time with her more than you actually do. You talk to her about the important things that are concerning you *before* you take your pants off, when you know you have her full and undivided attention. When she's doing something that doesn't quite feel right, you come right out and tell her! (Well, how else is she supposed to know?!)

I hear from couples all the time that they're having little or no sex at all because (wait for it) they just *don't feel like it.* Yes, they *don't feel like* having a wonderful sense of closeness, a powerful relief of tension and just a rocking good time with the person they've chosen to spend the rest of their life with. They'd rather surf Facebook or binge watch Netflix!

The problem, as I see it, is that we have romanticized the heck out of the act of intercourse.

I'm not saying it can't and shouldn't be explosively fabulous on occasion, but a vast majority of the time, sex can just be a few minutes of connecting with your spouse in a way that you literally can't connect with any other person on the planet. And ladies, if what I hear on a daily basis is true, you spend approximately ten times the effort coming up with ways to deflect sex than you'd have to spend actively engaging in the act.

(And for heaven's sake, please quit moaning about your thunder thighs or your flabby belly or any of your other perceived imperfections. Your man thinks you're gorgeous. Beyond gorgeous! You're absolutely irresistible to him. In case you hadn't noticed, your man doesn't exactly look like Adonis either, but you love him anyway! All the more reason he finds you so irresistible.)

Sometimes women wonder if there's something wrong with them because they're not walking around thinking about sex all day. In a nutshell: they beat themselves up because they don't feel like a man. Let's face it, all a man needs for sexual energy is oxygen. Whenever women watch TV or movies, they see the women on the screen who can't *wait* to have sex; the vixens who throw themselves at their lovers, tearing off their clothes in a fit of uncontrollable passion because they are burning so intensely!! Then the normal, everyday woman looks at herself and thinks something is terribly wrong since she doesn't have all these intense feelings before sex. But let's be practical here: A lot of women don't feel a big, burning *urge* before making love to their husbands. The truth is, a lot of women don't feel like doing it until *they are doing it*. (In the words of NIKE – just do it!)

For many years, sex experts would refer to something called the *sexual response cycle,* and it went like this: Desire, arousal, plateau, orgasm, resolution. It was taken as fact that in both sexes, a person felt the stirrings of interest first, then became aroused, and then did the deed. But fairly recently, a shocking (at least to researchers) discovery was made:

WOMEN ARE DIFFERENT THAN MEN.

In the majority of women, desire comes *after* arousal! Thus, when your spouse gives you that little eyebrow wiggle and says, "So do you want a piece of this?" you're likely to reply with all honesty, "Not really."

But if he nuzzles your neck a little bit, maybe gives you a nice shoulder rub or scratches your back for a few minutes, you might just find yourself wanting a piece of that.

As for those women on TV and in movies – the ones burning with passion and tearing off their lovers' clothes—remember this: They are actors. They are being *paid* to *act* that way! I'm pretty sure if your husband gave you several thousands of dollars each time before you had sex, that you could *act* that way too!

Look at it this way: I'm going to bet you're not giddy with excitement when you book that gynecologist appointment. But you do it because you know it's good for you, and it's what you do. To be clear, nobody is saying you should be engaging in perfunctory, love-less sex all day, every day. I'm just saying give the guy a chance to *get* you in the mood. Be open to it. Embrace it. Embrace *him*. Make a date for sex, and then show up ready to take your pants off with a smile.

MARK GUNGOR | JENNA MC CARTHY

Treat Him Like a Cab Driver

Treat Him Like a Dog

MARK GUNGOR | JENNA MC CARTHY

Treat Him Like a Cab Driver

One evening I came home late due to meetings. My wife had already eaten supper and was relaxing in the living room. She hadn't made anything for me, but that was due to 1) not being sure when I would be home and 2) knowing I don't like reheated food.

After exchanging some pleasantries about our days I asked, "Can you make me something to eat?" Playfully she replied, "Make it yourself - you're a big boy."

I immediately began to launch into my whiney man mode, hoping to change her mind and force her to my rescue, but she stood resolute. She'd had a busy day and had already cooked dinner once that evening.

Treat Him Like a Dog

Besides, she was sitting comfortably and not wanting to get up. She simply repeated her mantra, "You can do it - you're a grown man."

After some more whining, I finally accepted the fact that I was on my own. I decided on some eggs, mostly on account of the fact that the only thing I can make is... well... eggs.

I pulled out a pan, fired up the stove and cracked open some eggs. Within seconds my lovely wife was up off of her comfortable couch, as if the Lord had performed an amazing miracle by proclaiming, "Arise and walk!" She shot over by me, looked over my shoulder and began to bark out detailed instructions: "Well, don't use *that* pan," and "That's the wrong heat setting," and "Don't do it like that!"

Uuuugh. If there is one thing I have noticed about the mini-battles between men and women it is this: She not only wants you do to something - she wants you to do it **HER** way!

- You can't just fold the clothes - you must fold them *her* way.
- You can't just load the dishwasher - you must load it *her* way.

- You can't just mop the floor – you must mop it *her* way.
- You can't just do the laundry – you must... well, forget about it. My wife won't even let me touch the laundry!

And then women wonder, no – they cry aloud, "Why can't I get him to do things for me?!"

Really??

Look, you can tell him what you'd like done, or you can do it yourself. But don't put him in the loser position of being micromanaged. In a man's world, there's no third option of "Do it and let me tell you in painstaking detail exactly how it should be done."

When a man is at work and discovers he is constantly being micromanaged in excruciatingly painful detail, do you know what he does? He finds another job.

Why is this such a deal killer for men? Because we're *men!* We're built to be providers, caretakers, get-it-done dudes. We are not wired to be constantly reminded of what losers we are or how we fall short.

Do you know why your husband does what he does for a living? It is mostly likely due to the fact that it

Treat Him Like a Dog

is the *one* thing in his life that, when he does it, he is not criticized for it. In fact, he most likely wound up doing whatever it is he does because others *praised* him for how well he does it.

When you feel the need—and I know some of you feel it deeply and often—to constantly dip into your bottomless well of opinions on the Best Way to Do Absolutely Everything That Can Possibly Be Done, we feel like failures who are being subjected to repeated, sometimes daily, anesthesia-free neutering. And believe me when I say that most men, when being subjected to constant criticism, do not think, "Okay then, I'll work harder and do better." No, they think, "I don't think I'll do this anymore."

"That's not how you hold the baby." "*This* is the way you clean the toilet." "You fold the towels in thirds, not quarters." Unless your husband has a serious Oedipal complex, he's not going to like it when you act like his mother. (And do you really want to be your own mother-in-law? Think about that.)

I'll let you in on a little secret: We already *know* that you can do roughly everything in the universe that there is to do better than we can. This small fact is completely irrelevant to us. We're black-and-white, and you're fifty billion shades of gray. To us, a job is done when it's done; not when it's done to your exacting (read: exhausting) standards. And when you're waiting in the wings for us to do the World's Worst Job at something so you can remind us of your superior ways, do you know what you're going to get? I call it:

Stinking on purpose.

Oh yes, it's a real thing, and a useful one at that. See, we know if we ignore your step-by-step instructions and fold the dang towel in quarters, eventually you will get so fed up with refolding it that you'll just *do it yourself* and save us both that annoying step that involves us. Which, frankly, is sort of what we wanted all along.

Here's another little secret that could cost me my man-card but I nevertheless feel as if you should know: Us guys? Sometimes we feel like frauds. Like we're only *pretending* to be these big, strong, capable, competent *grown-up* men who know how to do everything (when secretly we're waiting to be exposed as dimwitted oafs). Even when we are succeeding at work, there is this haunting voice inside our heads that

Treat Him Like a Dog

says, "It's just a matter of time before they figure out you really don't know what you are doing."

So when you meticulously detail how you'd like us to, say, drive a car, or put together your new Ikea bookcase, or *fold a stinking towel,* we panic. "She's onto us!" we scream inside our otherwise mostly-empty heads. Then we do one of the two things men around the globe are famous for doing when they're cornered: We either 1) get ridiculously defensive and say a bunch of stupid things we'll regret immensely later, or 2) retreat into our silent and lonely man-caves until you seem significantly less annoyed. I probably don't need to point out that neither of these is a particularly pleasant outcome.

So now it's up to you to ask yourself: Do you passionately want your towels to be folded in perfect, symmetrical thirds, or do you simply want the *towels to be folded?* Because if it's the latter, shove that laundry basket right on over. You say it's the former? Well then, I hope you're prepared to fold towels all by your lonesome into eternity.

Despite their bravado, men have incredibly fragile egos. And rather than be humiliated in front of their wives, they would rather not try. Better to not even put in any effort at all (even though they know they'll be nagged at by their wives) than to try and fail and be shown to be a disappointment.

Want to know one of the biggest complaints I hear from women? It's that their husbands won't take the lead. Well girls, here is how you get a man to lead: You get out of the way! Do you want to know which women have husbands who cook? Those who don't tell their husbands how to cook. Know which women have husbands who clean? Those who don't tell their husbands how to clean. Know which women have husbands who fold laundry? Women who don't tell their husbands how to fold laundry.

One of the big knocks on churches is that their leadership tends to be overwhelmingly dominated by men. When I became a pastor I thought, "Not under my watch. I am an enlightened, cutting-edge guy. From now on we will have both husbands and wives serve in leadership positions! What could be better than to have both the male and female views at work together?"

Yes, I felt quite proud of myself, changing the status quo and showing that a woman can have as clear and strong a voice as a man.

Treat Him Like a Dog

What I discovered, however (much to my dismay), was this: When their wives were present, the men would sit quietly and say nothing. And I mean, absolutely and completely - nothing. Only the occasional guy would speak up and only when (it seemed to me) that he knew his wife would approve of what he was about to say.

I was stunned. Even I had to learn that in the world of men, they don't like to be embarrassed or be open to criticism in front of their wives. You see, most pastors have no problem speaking up. In fact, we live for the opportunity to stand in front of a crowd and impart our wisdom. But that is atypical for the world of men. According to studies, most men say their greatest fear is speaking in front of people. In fact, they say they fear it more than death! (I guess the worst thing would be for a man to be forced to give a speech before his own execution.) And as much as a man doesn't like opening himself to possible criticism with people in general, he *really* doesn't want to do it in front of his wife.

I eventually learned it was best to *not* have wives present in our meetings. When the wives were absent, an amazing and startling transformation took place: These very same men would speak up, become engaged and even (dare I say it?) lead. Oh, don't panic. We could still have a woman serve - just not with her husband. Because if the husband was present, he would say little to nothing, so great was his reluctance to be humbled in front of his wife.

All this reminds me of the following joke:

Two lines formed outside the gates of heaven. At the front of one line was a sign with the words: "Henpecked Husbands." The sign for the other line read: "Husbands Who Were Not Henpecked."

The line for the henpecked men went on as far as the eye could see. The other line had just one man standing in it.

Curious, the henpecked husbands asked him how he got in that line. The man replied, "My wife told me to stand here."

Which brings us at long last to our analogy of a cab driver...

Think, for a blessed, beautiful moment, how you treat your cab driver: He asks you where you want to go and you tell him. You don't map out his route or yell at

Treat Him Like a Dog

him for driving too fast, or accuse him of being a selfish, insensitive jerk with no regard for your hairdo when he rolls down his window. If he forgets to turn on his blinker, I'll bet you let it slide. You hop in and sit back and trust him to do his job and guess what? He probably gets you where you need to go every single time.

Try that with your husband: Have faith in his abilities and in his *capabilities*. Treat him like a man, not a boy. Hop in and sit back and trust him to do his job. He may not get you where you'd like to go every single time—he's human after all—but I can promise you, it'll be a far more enjoyable ride.

MARK GUNGOR | JENNA MC CARTHY

Treat Him Like a Dog

Treat Him Like a Child

I know, I know. I *just* got done telling you to treat him like a man, not a boy. And I meant every word of that. I'm certainly not about to suggest you start treating him *literally* like a child; I'm merely going to recommend that you make an effort, on occasion, to muster up even a fraction of the love, attention, affection, compassion, tenderness and forgiveness—yes, I said the dreaded f-word—that you show *your own* children easily and often.

Think about your kid for a second. (If you don't have children, picture a niece or nephew or a friend's child. Surely there's at least one rambunctious little whipper-snapper in your life you can conjure for these

Treat Him Like a Dog

purposes.) I'm going to guess that no matter how fabulous of a parent/aunt/Godparent/neighbor you are, this child frequently acts out, talks back, misbehaves, spills milk in your car, claims the biggest slice of pizza for himself or otherwise disappoints you. Let me ask you: Do you keep a running mental tab of these injustices, or mention them in front of his friends or yours, or bring them up when he gets gum in his hair for the *umpteenth time*? Of course you don't! Your love for him would never allow it. Besides, you are keenly aware that as a human being, it's his job to learn to make his way through the world—a task that simply cannot be done without a few slip-ups. Okay - a *lot* of slip-ups.

Well, guess what? We men are still learning, too! Albert Einstein, the original genius, said it best: "As soon as you stop learning, you start dying." And since I'm nowhere near ready to cash in my chips, you can expect me to keep learning (i.e. making lots and *lots* of mistakes) for the next few decades at least.

But back to your offspring. Think about how available you are to these precious fruits of your womb. Talk about a 24/7 job! You know that you will almost always drop whatever it is you're doing—cooking, cleaning, sleeping, sometimes breathing—when your children want your attention or affection. If they scrape a knee or burn a finger, you're there with the first aid kit before anyone can shout *who moved the ice pack????????* When their tiny, innocent feelings get hurt, you'd drive a steak into your own heart if you thought it would erase even a whisper of their pain. Without hesitation, you forego sleep and stay up the entire night nursing them through their cough, cold, runny nose and earache.

(Speaking of illness, you may have noticed how *some* of us guys turn into whiny, sniveling babies when we're sick. We shuffle-and-moan about the house leaving a trail of barely-used Kleenex in our wake. And do you want to know why? DO YOU? Because it's the one time—the single, solitary, lousy time—that we can. Do you think we don't want to whine and moan when we pay bills or shovel snow from the driveway or change a tire on the side of the dusty, eight-lane highway in the scorching sun? OF COURSE WE DO! But we keep it together, because we're supposed to. We *have* to.

So when we've got a raging ninety-nine degree fever, it's like God is giving us a hall pass to let down that macho guard for a day or two, three max. Do we

Treat Him Like a Dog

take advantage of this? Yes, sometimes we do. Do we want you to mop our brow and bring us hot tea and rub our feet and maybe, if you can spare the time, whip us up some homemade chicken soup? If it wouldn't be too much trouble, we'd enjoy that tremendously. And if all of that seems too much to ask, remember that when you find a garden snake in the garage and we promptly march out there with a shovel and a trash bag, you can bet your bottom we'll do it without a single sniffle. You're welcome.)

  Another reason we envy the way you treat the kids? The praise. Dear Lord, the praise! To hear you tell it, your children are prodigies. Geniuses, every last one of them! Every scribble they draw (ghastly), every off-tune song they sing (intolerable), every weed they pick for you (insignificant) is the most incredible thing you have ever seen, heard or smelled. You pay particular attention to their efforts and put a whole lot less emphasis on the outcomes. (The bedspread is crooked? Who cares! She made her bed! Let's get her a trophy!) And why do you bend over backwards to shower your charges with your approval and admiration? Why, you're building up their egos, of course! You want them to go out into the big, scary world filled with confidence and poise; with the belief that they are talented and honorable and above all, worthy of bottomless love.

Bet your husband wouldn't mind a booster shot of *that*. (Remember the pathetically fragile male ego I mentioned earlier? Ahem.)

But here's what your spawn are getting from you that we husbands deeply, passionately desire above all else: When they make mistakes—big or small, intentional or accidental, miniscule or mind-blowing—you forgive them, easily and immediately. (Sure, you might dole out a consequence, but it is always, and I mean *always*, doled out with a sincere feeling of *this hurts me more than it hurts you*.) Can you imagine holding a ten year grudge against your child, or withholding affection for days at a stretch to 'teach him a lesson'? Those things would be unthinkable! Instead, when he blunders you simply tell him that he can do better, and in return he promises to try.

Accept, forgive, comfort, encourage, console - all without keeping a running list of transgressions? I don't know about you, but that sounds like a dreamy setup to me.

Love keeps no record of wrongs.

- 1 Corinthians 13:5 NIV

MARK GUNGOR | JENNA MC CARTHY

Treat Him Like a Personal Trainer

Treat Him Like a Dog

Treat Him Like a Personal Trainer

Don't have a personal trainer? Then your water aerobics instructor or Zumba teacher or heck, even your dental hygienist will do for these purposes. We're far from elitist over here. I just want you to picture the person who gets you to do something on a quasi-regular basis that frankly you'd very much rather not.

Let's go with the trainer, just so we're not mixing our metaphors here: She pushes you, taunts you, barks commands at you, and drags your rear end out of bed at unholy hours. She makes you wear *body hugging Spandex*, for crying out loud. In public! But still you show up week after week, dressed and ready to do what she asks of you, even though you know it's going to hurt like

Treat Him Like a Dog

nobody's business and ruin your hair for the rest of the day and you may or may not be able to lift your arms above your head tomorrow. And why do you put up with her pushing? Because in your extremely wise heart of hearts, you know it's going to make you a better, stronger person. *She's going to make you a better, stronger person.* (Yeah, yeah, you're going to do the work... but she's lighting the fire and you both know it!) If you wanted to stay home and lie on the couch and eat potato chips all day every day and she let you, she'd be the worst personal trainer on the planet... am I right?

    I'm going to hope that your husband doesn't taunt you, bark commands at you or drag you out of bed... but make no mistake: There's a reason you married the man you did, and I'd bet my last nickel it wasn't because he's handy with barbecue tools or knows how to make sense of your ridiculously complicated tax return. It wasn't even his dashing good looks or his big, fat bank account that sealed the deal for you. No, I'm going to propose that you married him because he *challenges* you—a fact that felt impossibly intoxicating while you were dating and now, sometimes, makes you want to set your hair on fire and run screaming into the street from the sheer, overwhelming frustration of it all.

We all do this: We pick someone totally different from us. It makes sense - who wants to marry themselves? It is a true statement that opposites attract. But the reason opposites attract is not because we all carry a secret wish to be tortured by another. No, we are drawn to someone who has what we don't have. This is because we *need* what they have. For example: It is the joining of opposite parts that makes sex such a unique and wonderful experience. (While not intending to insult anyone, as a true heterosexual, I've got to say: I ain't interested in what I've already got.) But this goes far beyond just physical parts - it includes the mental, emotional, even spiritual parts that we lack. It is in the combining of all of these differences that we find the promise of fulfillment. It is also the precise thing that dives us crazy! For despite the siren call of *viva la difference*, make no mistake, all marital arguments can be boiled down to one very simple argument: Why can't you be more like me?!

And while his many differences can at times be maddening (please don't take offense when I say this, because I say it not just with love but also with a

Treat Him Like a Dog

hearty chuckle): *You picked him!* More importantly, you *didn't* pick the guy who agreed with every last thing you said—and surely there were at least a handful of them—or answered your every, "Where should we eat/stay/sit?" query with, "Wherever you'd like, dear." You willingly, eagerly even, agreed to spend the rest of your days on this glorious earth living side-by-side with this one man whose job it seems is to disagree with you, want something you don't, and generally push your every last button.

Note to Alanis Morissette: Now *that's* ironic.

He likes westerns; you prefer rom-coms. He's a saver; you're a spender. He craves Italian (all those carbs!); you pine for Thai food (so spicy!). He wants sex *all the flipping time* (according to you); you *never* want it (according to him). Oh, opposites attract all right! And then they spend the better part of their days butting heads. Which truly, in my rarely humble opinion, is a magnificent and substantial gift.

I know, you think I'm nuts. But remember, if we aren't growing, we're dying. If we're not being challenged, we're stagnating. If nobody ever showed us a different way of seeing or doing something, we'd all wither away and perish standing at the bottom of a broken escalator or clinging to a lounge cushion from our sunken ship. If we want to survive, we listen to the voices around us who see or know something other than what we do.

Run up the stairs! SWIM!!! YOU CAN DO IT! There's no "I" in TEAM, girls. And teamwork makes the dream work. (Call the Corny Police if you must, but honestly, sometimes husbands and wives seem to forget they're *on the same team!*)

Remember, nobody ever said marriage was going to be easy. (If it was easy, they'd call the whole darn thing a honeymoon!) And because you didn't go and do something crazy like marry yourself, chances are you find your wedded selves at odds as often as not. You argue about what time the kids should go to bed, where to go for dinner, when it's time to buy a new car. Even when the facts are inarguable, you *still* argue. (Him: "We NEVER have sex! Twice a week if I'm lucky." Her: "We have sex ALL THE TIME. At least twice a week!" Him: "It's sweltering in here! It must be seventy-five degrees!" Her: "It's freezing in here! It must be seventy-five degrees!")

Treat Him Like a Dog

At the risk of pointing out the blazingly obviously, *you're different people!* Instead of getting exasperated by your polarity, look at it this way: You each bring something valuable to the table. Together, you are far stronger and more effective than you could ever be individually. You balance each other out! Imagine if every homebody married a homebody, or every tightwad married a tightwad. B-O-R-I-N-G, right? We pick partners who compliment us, test us, challenge our thinking and help us grow. (But not partners who "complete us," no matter what that Tom Cruise says. You are not a three legged table or a violin without a bow! You're a perfectly imperfect creature of God. Just so we're clear.) There's a saying I love: "The happiest couples never have the same character; they just have the best understanding of their differences."

Exercise gurus like to say, "The pain you feel today is the strength you'll feel tomorrow." (Which is really just a fancier way of saying 'no pain, no gain,' but it's still true!) Take that sentiment to heart and try this in your marriage: Put on your (metaphorical) Spandex and show up ready to be challenged, to learn and to become a better person. Don't just be open to your differences; *embrace* them. Be ready to do the hard work you know is necessary for growth. Then thank your spouse for his role in the awesomeness that is your winning team.

MARK GUNGOR | JENNA MC CARTHY

Treat Him Like Your Phone

Treat Him Like a Dog

Treat Him Like Your Phone

Come on, admit it: You adore that little glowing, buzzing, dinging device. You love to gaze into its magical face. You delight in having it near you, or preferably *on you*, at all times. You'll stay up far past your bedtime for a few extra hours of exploring its hidden treasures. *What man wouldn't want some of that action?*

And boy, does that wireless wonder of yours have you wrapped around its little antenna! You could be in the shower, performing a circus tightrope act or dead asleep; if that thing rings, you jump. You reach for it at every stoplight, during every commercial break and sometimes, secretly, during dinner or in the middle of a movie. You wouldn't dream of going to the bathroom

Treat Him Like a Dog

without it, and when you can't find it for thirty seconds straight, you are flooded with panic.

Admit it: if you realized two-hundred miles into your cross-country road trip that you'd left the thing at home, what would you do? You'd turn around and retrieve it without a second's hesitation. You'd *have* to! How on earth would you find the closest Starbucks or upload your amazing vacation photos to Facebook without it?

There's a time and a place for everything, and the time and place to be on your phone most definitely isn't *all day every day everywhere you go.* And make no mistake, guys are just as guilty as gals when it comes to their phones. But change has to start somewhere, and there's a good chance if you lead, he'll follow.

This isn't so much about marriage as it is about *manners.* Picture yourself sitting at a fancy restaurant... yeah, yeah, the French one he never wants to go to. Just as you're mid-way through your detailed explanation of precisely how you'd like the chef to prepare your meal (you'd prefer the spinach steamed, not sautéed, with the béchamel sauce *on the side...*) you lose your server's attention.

"Hang on a sec," he tells you, not looking at you, index finger poised. "Just gotta reply to this email..."

Or imagine you've forked over an obscene amount of money for center-row orchestra seats to the Tony-winning Broadway musical of your dreams. (Obviously you're there with your best girlfriend, because there's no way you're dragging your guy to one of those! But I digress.) You're riveted by the magical voice of the handsome lead actor when he abruptly stops singing mid-refrain, pulls his cell phone from his pocket and starts pecking away at the screen. "Just have to text my brother back really quickly. Oh, and look. Overstock has free shipping through Sunday and I need a new bathmat. Sorry, where was I?"

These things are unthinkable because they would be totally and ridiculously rude. And yet thanks to our ubiquitous cell phones, we're all rude all the dang time! They beep, chime, ding, or ring and more often than not we stop whatever it is we're doing to see what the latest emergency is. (Your Target order has shipped! Release the doves and sound the alarms!)

Can I let you in on a little secret? Unless it's a call from a stranded child or a sick elderly relative, *it can*

Treat Him Like a Dog

almost always wait! People come before screens. We survived for thousands of years without technological tethers, and I think we've all forgotten that sometimes, it was actually pretty nice to be occasionally unavailable. I mean, you could hunker down in a movie theater, just you and your date and your trough of popcorn, and disappear into a delicious story. Now we're only ever half-present everywhere we go, endlessly distracted by checking email or snapping photos or Googling "What did Meg Ryan look like before plastic surgery?"

Like I said, men can be as bad (or even worse) when it comes to their handheld virtual lovers, but this is not a contest to see who can be more rude or insensitive to each other. And besides, as my mother used to ask us, "If your friend jumps off a cliff are you going to do the same?"

Come on, this is a pretty simple one. If you responded to your man the way you respond to your phone, life with him could be dramatically improved.

MARK GUNGOR | JENNA MC CARTHY

Treat Him Like a Stranger

Treat Him Like a Dog

MARK GUNGOR | JENNA MC CARTHY

Treat Him Like a Stranger

Think about the random people you encounter throughout any given day and how you interact with them for a second. Chances are you're friendly, cordial and above all, so gracious it hurts. You ask the cashier at Starbucks how his day is going; compliment your server on her cute shoes; signal the driver across from you at the four-way stop sign to go ahead of you, even though it's obvious to you both that you were there first. You do all of this with a smile, and maybe even a twinkle in your eye. Most of us treat perfect strangers more kindly than the people we profess to love the most!

And why is this? Because we're human! We take our most precious blessings for granted all day long,

Treat Him Like a Dog

every darned day. Shelter, love, education, electricity, clean water, food, freedom: These are all things that you likely have even though countless others don't, and yet you probably rarely if ever stop to appreciate them.

The same can be true when it comes to your husband: He's there. Big whoop. (He also left whiskers in the bathroom sink yesterday and he didn't even notice your new haircut.)

Except it is a big whoop. It's a huge whoop, in fact. You committed your entire life to this person; the least you can do is muster up an occasional unsolicited smile or spontaneous compliment, or set down the laundry basket when he asks for a hug.

Strangers are easy to be nice to because there's no history there. There's no lingering resentment over the dinner date they didn't plan, the love note they didn't write or the bed they didn't make. Without the weight of the bottomless business of running a home, raising children and juggling dual careers, you can actually have a quick and lively discussion about the weather or a friendly debate over paper-versus-plastic.

As I travel all over the word, speaking to thousands of people in my conferences, I often hear people say, "We really love you!" Nice to hear, but I always respond, "You love me because you don't really know me. The closer I get, the harder I am to love..."

You know another reason it's easy to be nice to strangers? Because we sort of have to. We were raised to be polite and kind in public. We're not wolves, as our mothers were fond of pointing out. Plus, we actually care about what strangers think of us! To that end, think about how you react when your kid misbehaves at home... versus when he has a full-blown, on-the-floor temper tantrum in Target. At home, you might (on occasion, at least) turn into a shrieking, blood-curdling banshee, but in Target? "Come on, my sweet little angel, Mommy needs you to stop screaming, okay? Be a good boy and quiet down so you don't pierce the eardrums of all of the nice shoppers. I'll buy you a toy if you stop. Yes, the life-size ride-on pony. And the entire Lego village. There, there, that's a good, quiet boy..." Because heaven forbid those shoppers think you're raising an ill-behaved child!

Have you ever been in the middle of an argument or a stand-off with your spouse and had the phone ring? I have, and I'm here to tell you it's an eye-opening

Treat Him Like a Dog

experience. This woman who only seconds ago was hissing at me like an angry snake snatches that phone up and trills into it with a voice that could have come out of an angel or Snow White herself. "Helloooooooo?" she sings sweetly, and the skies open up and birds begin to chirp and all you can think is "Oh, sure, try to pretend that you're nice! Nobody would believe it for a second if they saw you thirty seconds ago!" (They wouldn't think the arguing guy was very nice either.)

  This is an actual trick that psychologists use, and I'll admit it's more than a little bit cruel… but it's also remarkably effective: Imagine for a brief moment—as vividly as you can—that your husband has been taken from you unexpectedly. (Yup, dead. Gone. Forever. I told you this was cruel!) Sit with that feeling for a moment. Now ask yourself: Right now, when you're experiencing that profound sense of loss, does it matter in the absolute least that he occasionally misses the hamper when he plays boxerball or frequently fails to nestle his sock drawer into its fully closed position? (Two things, incidentally, that women complain about all the time.) How big a deal is it, really, that he insists on exclusive operation rights to the remote control, or occasionally forgets to call to tell you he'll be home late? Would you give your left arm for the chance to endure any of these "injustices" even one more time? Studies actually show that when you intensely imagine losing someone you love, it can reignite feelings of gratitude and appreciation toward them practically instantaneously. (If you found yourself fantasizing about turning his home office into a sewing room should he meet his tragic and untimely demise, you might want to seek professional help. I'm just saying.)

When you're about to unleash on your man, ask yourself: Would I say what I'm about to say—in the tone and at the volume I'm about to use—to a stranger on the street? Or even in front of one? Sure, it's natural to lose it on occasion with our nearest and dearest; they're supposed to be there for us no matter what; for better or for worse. We're allowed to show them our worst selves, because they'll keep loving us anyway and sometimes we urgently need an outlet for our rage and exasperation. But has common courtesy left the building of your marriage entirely?

Envision this scenario: Your brand new neighbor

stopped over to introduce herself. After she's gone, you realize she left her sweater behind. Would you slam open the door and run out angrily, shaking your fist and shouting insults at her, ("I bet you'd forget your head if it weren't screwed on!") or would you trot after her with a smile and a kind word? ("It was great to meet you, I hope you'll come back soon!") Or picture yourself running errands at your typical frantic pace when you bump into an old childhood friend. She stops and throws her arms out, ready to embrace you. Do you a) immediately forget the silly string of tasks you were so intent upon and hug the life out of her before spending a few minutes catching up, or b) put up your hands as if to block her and say, "Sorry hon, I've really got to get these books back to the library, maybe we can chat later?"

    Women and men frequently yearn for their early courtship days, when everyone was nice and always on their best behaviors. Every once in a while, when you can muster up the enthusiasm, be that woman again. This isn't about bowing down to his needs, but leading by example. When you do that, I promise you that incredibly good things will follow.

MARK GUNGOR | JENNA MC CARTHY

BONUS CHAPTER!

Do NOT Treat Him Like Your Girlfriend

Treat Him Like a Dog

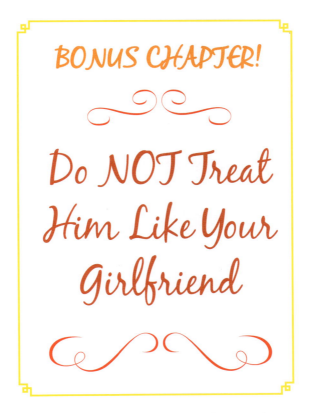

BONUS CHAPTER!

Do NOT Treat Him Like Your Girlfriend

As I said in the beginning, if you ask most women to describe their ideal man and then listen closely, invariably, they will describe another woman.

"Someone who likes to take long walks…"

"Someone who loves to share their feelings…"

"Someone who enjoys going shopping…"

Look, men can make great men, but we make *terrible* girlfriends.

Treat Him Like a Dog

I was being interviewed on a famous Christian radio program. At one point the woman who was conducting the interview said, "Mark, don't you believe a man should meet all of the emotional needs of his wife?" Keep in mind this was not really a question – it was a set-up, much like in volleyball where one player pops the ball up so their teammate can slam it down on the opposing side. I could just sense her delight as she expected me to punch it hard on why a man should be the consummate emotional outlet for his wife.

"Do I think a man should meet all of the emotional needs of his wife?" I repeated. "Of course not!"

She looked at me in astonishment and shouted, "What?!?"

I explained to her that there is not a man on earth designed to meet *all* of the emotional needs of a woman. But sadly, that is the absurd conventional wisdom that is being battered around by many relationship experts today.

Good grief. No wonder so many women who buy into this nonsense are so miserable. They marry some poor unsuspecting soul, stick a straw into his brain, and then proceed to suck the life out of him, trying to get him to fulfill *all* of their emotional needs. But he can't. And, furthermore, he is not supposed to.

"Then what should I do?" is the frequent cry.

My reply:

"*For the love of God get some friends!!*"

And as soon as you accuse him of being uncommunicative and unresponsive, do you know what happens? (Of course you do! This isn't your first rodeo.)

He shuts down even more!

Remember: Point out to a man that he is consistently failing at something and he will most likely stop trying entirely. It's all part of that fragile ego thing we have been talking about. And the reality is, it's not true that he never talks to you, it's simply that he doesn't necessarily want to discuss at great length and in painstaking detail every waking minute of your day.

Most men like to summarize. Many women like to relive events in excruciatingly painful detail. In fact, it frequently takes her more time to retell any given event

Treat Him Like a Dog

than it actually took for the event to happen in the first place! It's like the scene in "The Princess Bride" when the evil villain Rugen connects poor Westly to a time device that sucks the life out of him, which results in his ending up "mostly dead."

Look, I think it is fine for you to take a minute to describe what only took a second to transpire, just don't do it with your husband. Find a girlfriend, a sister, your mom – heck, even *his* mom. Just don't get angry that your husband makes a really lousy girlfriend.

I am certain that on some level, you realize this. But your need to share these things is so great that you occasionally lose sight of *his* needs and desires and you launch your verbal assault anyway. Then you proceed to get furious when his eyes glaze over and he not-so-subtly tunes you out.

Naturally, you take his reaction personally. *If he loved you, he'd listen to you! He'd be interested in what you have to say, and he'd engage in the lengthy, animated discourse your heart so desires!*

You believe this with every fiber in your being, too. The only problem is, you're dead wrong. Your husband walks in the door and you start to regale him with the particulars of your beloved dog's visit with the vet: "Well, I took Delilah to the doctor and guess what? She's got worms... and she needs her teeth cleaned, which she doesn't like to have done, but she *needs* to have it done, though she probably won't be happy, and you can't just let her teeth fall out because that would be cruel and do you think a dog can survive without teeth? I think not! I mean, teeth are very important to a dog, and besides, it could help with her dog breath, which is pretty bad. Don't you think??" Of course, as soon as you ask, "Don't you think?" he panics because all he heard you say was something about a doctor and a dog.

Does he love Delilah any less than you do? Maybe; maybe not. But even if he loved her fifty times more, he's a bottom-line kind of guy; always has been and always will be. "Delilah needs her teeth cleaned" is all of the information he needs (and fine, maybe how much it's going to cost), much to your chagrin.

Is he happy that you talked to your sister today? Sure! Happy wife, happy life! Is he interested in hearing a play-by-play of the conversation that actually lasts twice as long as the call itself did? I can't emphasize this

Treat Him Like a Dog

enough when I say *not in the least.*

There's a saying: "If you always do what you always did, you'll always get what you always got." So while you *could* continue to attempt to capture his interest with ever-more riveting and exhaustive accounts of your every endeavor, you also could try talking to him *his* way. You could face the fact that he loves you deeply and also he's just not interested in hearing a real-time recap of your latest dream or email exchange. "Had a funny dream" or "Emailed your mom today" is all the information he requires. If he wants to know more, he'll ask! (I wouldn't suggest holding your breath.)

Now, if you actually follow through with that advice, you will likely have somewhere in the neighborhood of four or five million thoughts, feelings and random musings floating about in your head on a daily basis, desperate to escape. *Now what are you going to do?* Well, if you liked to sing, you'd join a chorus. If you wanted to tango, you'd find a dance studio. So like I said, if want to re-live the micro-events of your life to an enthusiastic audience, *get yourself some girlfriends!*

Unlike your husband, your girlfriends *do* want to hear all about the dirty look the cashier at Macy's gave you when you tried to use an expired coupon. They'll lean in intently to catch every word of your whispered tale of your crazy neighbor's latest shenanigans. You say you just finished a fabulous novel? Share! Tell! Dissect! Your female friends will eat up every last word. They make *great* girlfriends – because they are actually girls!

Likewise, when you ask your husband how his day was, please understand that to him, this question (like most, frankly) only requires a one-word answer: fantastic, great, good, okay, lousy. Expecting him to delight you with a flowery account of his last ten hours would be like hoping he'll notice you're wearing a new dress or parted your hair on the opposite side. In other words, *about seventeen hundred miles from* likely.

With that in mind, I beg you: Don't equate his short-windedness with a lack of love. Stop getting frustrated by his "inability to communicate" and instead try to speak his language on occasion. Accept the fact that he prefers answers to stories, and reserve the latter for your gal pals. Do this and he will adore you forever. (Silently, of course.)

More Treats

We hope you enjoyed TREAT HIM LIKE A DOG and that you feel like it's given you a fun new way to approach living with your husband.

If you know a man who is looking to employ some of the same simple, enjoyable strategies with his wife, or you want to know how to TREAT the children in your life, we've got you covered:

For *him*, there's TREAT HER LIKE A TRUCK. For parents, there's TREAT THEM LIKE MONKEYS.

We're including the introductions to each on the following pages, so you'll have an idea of what's in store. Why not TREAT yourself? Here's to happily ever after!

markgungor.com

More from Gungor Publishing

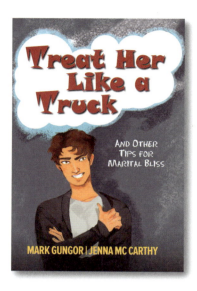

Introduction

Congratulations! You're now the proud owner of a book on relationships. I'll bet this has been on your wish list for years, possibly decades. Is that the sound of you tap-dancing I hear? Or was that a champagne cork popping? After all, the only thing men love even more than talking about their feelings is reading about them, am I right?

I'll be here all week!

Obviously, I jest. The fact that you've gotten to this third paragraph, frankly, could be considered one of those "everyday miracles" some

markgungor.com

folks use to prove God exists. So, let me tell you right up front that even though this technically is a relationship book, I promise you it's unlike any other you've ever encountered—or more likely, any you've dreaded encountering. For one thing, I'm not going to give you painful exercises to perform or ask you to delve deep into your psyche/past/wallet to figure out why you're so emotionally constipated. Besides, explaining why a man is emotionally constipated is pretty easy: It's because you're a man! It's how God designed you, and I'm pretty sure he had a darned good reason for doing it that way. Likewise, he designed your wife the way she is for a reason, too, which may or may not be slightly neater, fresher-smelling and needier than you are, emotionally and conversationally.

Did God construct men craving high speeds in a car with rolled-down windows and give women blinding white knuckles and the skills to create complicated hairstyles that immediately fall apart when said window is rolled down just so we could drive each other insane until death finally separates us? No, these differences were never designed to drive us crazy. He designed us differently so we could complement one another; learn from and grow with; someone who makes us whole.

And then drives us nuts.

Why do we do this thing called marriage? Why are we so powerfully drawn to someone so different from ourselves, even though at times it can be so completely frustrating?

Well, beyond the obvious reason of sexual attraction, the truth is, we are better with that woman than we are without her.

The wise King Solomon once wrote:

Two are better than one, because they have
a good return for their labor:
If either of them falls down,
one can help the other up.
But pity anyone who falls
and has no one to help them up.
Also, if two lie down together, they will
keep warm.
But how can one keep warm alone?
Though one may be overpowered,
two can defend themselves.

Treat Her Like a Truck

If you're like most men, you probably feel like you're a pretty good husband, all things considered. You're not perfect, but you definitely love your wife, and you're certainly committed to her. So why does it sometimes feel like you can't make her happy?

The ironic answer is, because you're married to her!

See, if you'd intended to remain a bachelor for the rest of ever, my "how to be happy" advice would be completely different. I'd tell you to go ahead and fart in the car with the windows up, drink properly chilled bottles of beer while you watch ESPN around the clock, and let your nose hairs grow down to your chin if you happen to like that look. I would give you permission to never, ever watch another chick flick as long as you live, and encourage you to drag your hamper to the curb and start leaving your dirty boxers and socks scattered about your home like confetti. But if you're reading this book (and by that, I probably mean if your wife is making you read this book), I'd bet my last nickel you're no bachelor—or if you are, you won't be one for long. No, you are half of a

Treat Her Like a Truck

whole, and you've got someone else to think about now. Someone else with ideas, wants, needs, and movie preferences vastly different from your own. And it may be a fuzzy memory today, but when you stood before that altar or beside those gently lapping waves on that blinding white beach of your bride's wedding-destination dreams, you said some version of the following:

"I promise to love, honor and cherish you in sickness and in health, for richer or for poorer, for better or for worse, till death do us part."

(You did! You said that!)

As it turns out, till death do us part is a really looooong time—and being a loving, honoring, cherishing partner all day every day is no easy feat. In fact, by most accounts it borders on the impossible. Not to mention that living with another person (which typically means sharing the same bed, the same bathroom and the same thermostat) has been known to try even the most temperate of tempers.

If you're among the very blessed, you're not bickering about the Big Things (namely money, sex and kids) on a daily basis. Most married couples admit that more often than not they find themselves arguing about tiny, trivial matters.

Solomon also once wrote:

A quarrelsome wife is like the dripping of a leaky roof in a rainstorm.

- Proverbs 27:15 (NIV)

Granted, that was written from a man's perspective and there is conveniently no mention of the major pain in the rear that a husband can be, but the image of a dripping, leaky roof pretty much summarizes what life can be like after the "I Dos" have echoed off into the distant horizon.

I bet you'd like to plug that leak, wouldn't you? I bet you'd give up your favorite hobby for, like six months, maybe even a year, to have an airtight wife.

Here's the thing: You can! And it's not even that hard!

You: Oh, here you go. You're going to tell me I have to change.

Me: No I'm not. I'm really, truly not.

You: Mark, I don't believe you! How can I make my wife happy without changing? She doesn't even like me!

Of course, you're skeptical. I don't blame you, especially if you're married to a woman who occasionally or even frequently points out how miserable you make her. (All women do this, incidentally. Oh, they don't do it to be mean; they do it because they like to communicate. And they actually believe that if they tell us something they don't like about our personalities or behavior, that we'll actually change it! Bless their innocent, hopeful little hearts...) But you really can make her happy, and you can do it simply by continuing to do what you've done all along...with every other person and thing in your life.

Think about that lovely little lady you married for a minute. Sure, you love her, in the vague and all-encompassing sense of the word. You honor her (especially when she makes flank steak or doesn't turn down your request for a little morning action.) You try your best to cherish her, even when she insists on giving you a real-time play by play of her day when all you asked was how it was, and all you wanted to hear was "great." But you know it and I know it: You don't always appreciate her—and she certainly doesn't always get the best version of you.

Don't tell her I said this, but sometimes she's sort of like that hideous recliner chair you love so much. She's comfortable, she's dependable, and you probably wouldn't even notice if somebody spilled a bowl of chili on her. (Okay, you probably would notice that...and post a picture of it on Facebook.) But in a nutshell, you mostly take her for granted.

You: You lied! You said I didn't have to change!

Me: Relax. I didn't lie. You really don't have to change.

The super-easy-secret-trick to making your wedded wife happy is to behave the way you've always behaved—around your car, your television, your tool box, even your old baseball glove. I know, you think I sound crazy right now, but that's not important. What's important is that you're reading a relationship book, and you're enjoying it, and you're going to keep reading it because you have my word that you do not have to change.

markgungor.com

Treat Her Like a Truck

All you have to do is start treating her less like your old recliner and more like some of the other things in life that you love. It really is that easy.

Let's do this.

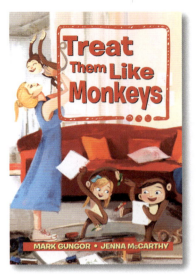

Introduction

There's an old saying by comedienne Phyllis Diller I like to misquote from time to time:

> "You spend the first twelve months of your kid's life teaching them to walk and talk, and the next twelve years telling them to sit down and shut up."

I say "misquote" because as I understand it, Phyllis originally said 'you spend the next twelve *months* telling them to sit down and shut up,' but I don't know anybody who managed to get a child to do either of those things in one measly year!

I'm going to tell you something you may not know about me: Of all the things I have been woefully unprepared for in this life—and lo, there have been many—I'd have to put that baffling, exhausting, head-banging phenomenon known as *parenthood* at the tippy top of the list.

No joke: I cannot count the times over the years that my late wife Debbie and I, during our parenting years, looked back and forth from our spawn to each other in genuine confusion and muttered, "Whose idea was this anyway?"

Let's be real about something: It's not like any of us passed any sort of Parental Fitness Test before we decided to start popping out puppies. And speaking of puppies, have you ever tried to adopt one—an unwanted, unwashed one from the pound even? If you haven't, I'm here to tell you that it *is not a fleeting endeavor.* Seriously. There are piles of paperwork and mandatory medical tests and "rehoming fees" and sometimes a waiting period and occasionally even a home inspection to determine if you and your household meet the appropriate minimum standards of "pet-parent suitability."

Oh yes, I know people who have been *denied doggy ownership* because their jobs were too demanding, their yards were too small, or there were other critters in the house that the adoption agency deemed "incompatible." Man, that must be embarrassing...Rejected because one's lifestyle is beneath that of a dog? Not dog-worthy?? Really?!?

But if you want to *make a brand-new human being from scratch* and then bring it home to your filthy, rat-infested shoebox of an apartment and proceed to leave it alone for extended periods of time while you travel around your neighborhood selling crystal meth? Knock yourself out! *Nobody is even going to try to stop you!* (Well, if you get caught you'll eventually go to prison, but I'm saying there are no prerequisites.)

And when you consider the fact that these *brand new human beings* are the result of a very enjoyable romp under the covers *(or wherever you do it)* that has nothing at all to do with *bottles and burp cloths and eventual college tuitions*, it's no wonder so many of us are at a loss when it comes to this whole business of child-rearing.

And the family culture we live in today only exacerbates the problem. You see, for thousands upon thousands of years of human experience, people lived around family. Most people lived their entire lives within a few miles of where they were born.

The result: You were constantly surrounded by people who had a vested interest in you and your offspring. A simple walk out the door and you were going to encounter a grandparent, uncle, aunt, or multiple cousins. One of the positives of all that familial interaction was that you were never more than a stone's throw away from people who loved you, who wanted to help you at all costs, and most importantly, who had lots of experience birthing and raising babies.

But that's not the case in our culture today. No, no, no! As soon as feasible, many of us move as far away from our families as conceivably possible. This is great for one's independence, but not so great for marriage and family. Because in this mobile, modern world, *you are on your own*. And when your toddler is coughing and crying all night long, your eight-year-old is struggling in math, or your demon-possessed teenager is getting into constant trouble at school...well, you will quickly learn that being "on your own" is a scary, lonely place indeed. *(A personal word of advice: Live as close to at least one set of grandparents as you can. Having experienced hands nearby can dramatically reduce your chance of self-inflicted harm brought on by mind-numbing offspring syndrome. This also makes for great, cost-free babysitters.)*

Parenting today? It's madness, all of it! Thankfully we do it anyway, or else this planet would be a sad and desolate place and we'd have nobody to come visit us in the nursing home one day.

> **LIVE AS CLOSE TO AT LEAST ONE SET OF GRANDPARENTS AS YOU CAN.**

All of which is to say, if you're bewildered by your babies in particular or puzzled by parenting in general, you are far from alone—and isolation isn't the only issue we face as families. Another part of the problem is this pervasive idea of the "perfect parent" the media is always trying to sell us. I will let you in on a secret here, friends:

THERE iS NO SUCH THiNG AS A PERFECT PARENT.

There are plenty of loving parents, and lots of well-read parents, and more than a few patience-of-Job parents, *but not one of them is perfect.* And the beauty of that is, it's okay! We don't *need* to be perfect! Our job as parents is to guide and instruct, and even as we're failing miserably, we're doing exactly that. ("Here's how *not* to do it, kids!")

That said, whether you're in the trenches with a newborn or walking around on eggshells around a surly teen, within these pages we've laid out a simple, sensible plan for raising fine, upstanding future adults (and keeping your own sanity and sense of humor intact). It starts with *treating them like monkeys.*

Really.

You're going to love it.

More Books by Gungor Publishing

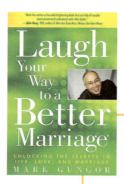

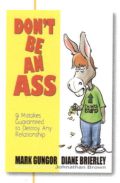
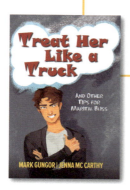

markgungor.com

More Books by Gungor Publishing

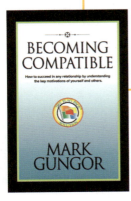
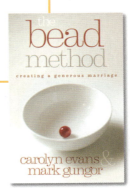

markgungor.com